Pebble®

How Fruits and Vegetables Grow

Tomatoes
Grow on a Vine

by Mari Schuh

Consulting Editor: Gail Saunders-Smith, PhD

Consultant: Sarah Pounders, education specialist
National Gardening Association

D1249329

CAPSTONE PRESS
a capstone imprint

Pebble Books are published by Capstone Press,
151 Good Counsel Drive, P.O. Box 669, Mankato, Minnesota 56002.
www.capstonepub.com

Library of Congress Cataloging-in-Publication Data
Schuh, Mari C., 1975–
  Tomatoes grow on a vine / by Mari Schuh.
    p. cm.—(Pebble books. How fruits and vegetables grow)
  Summary: "Simple text and photographs describe how tomatoes grow on vines"—
Provided by publisher.
  Includes bibliographical references and index.
  ISBN 978-1-4296-5278-0 (library binding)
  ISBN 978-1-4296-6187-4 (paperback)
  ISBN 978-1-4296-6858-3 (saddle-stitched)
  1. Tomatoes—Juvenile literature. I. Title. II. Series: Pebble (Mankato, Minn.). How
fruits and vegetables grow.
  SB349.S35 2011
  635'.642—dc22   2010025473

Note to Parents and Teachers

The How Fruits and Vegetables Grow set supports national science
standards related to life science. This book describes and illustrates
how tomatoes grow on vines. The images support early readers in
understanding the text. The repetition of words and phrases helps
early readers learn new words. This book also introduces early
readers to subject-specific vocabulary words, which are defined in
the Glossary section. Early readers may need assistance to read some
words and to use the Table of Contents, Glossary, Read More, Internet
Sites, and Index sections of the book.

Printed in the United States of America in North Mankato, Minnesota
042011
006140

Table of Contents

Author's Note

In this book, we refer to tomatoes as vegetables. Some scientists classify tomatoes as fruits because tomatoes have seeds. Other people call tomatoes vegetables because they are cooked and eaten like many vegetables, such as in salads and as parts of a main meal.

Vines in the Garden

On the ground or up
a fence, vines grow longer
each day. Many fruits
and vegetables grow
on garden vines.

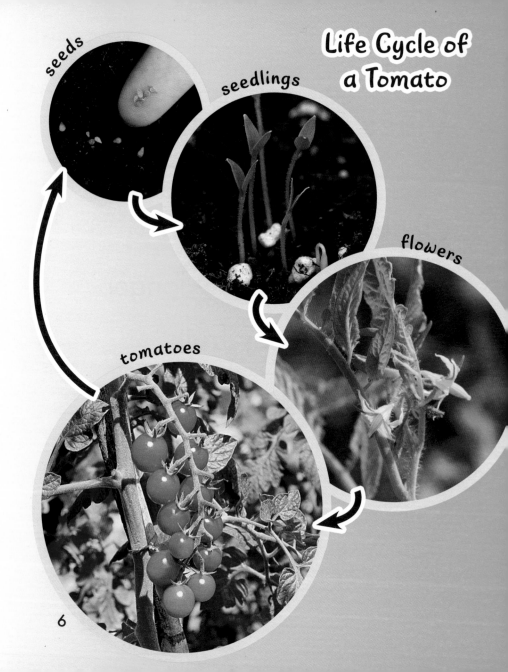

Life Cycle of a Tomato

seeds

seedlings

flowers

tomatoes

Tomatoes are vegetables
that grow on vines.
Tomato vines climb up
tall stakes or wire cages.

Growing

Tomato vines start as seeds. The seeds sprout in about one week. Loose soil gives roots room to grow.

branch

leaves

10

The seeds grow into seedlings with many branches and leaves.

Pollination

As tomato vines grow,
small yellow flowers form.
Each flower has pollen
and eggs inside. The pollen
fertilizes the eggs.

After fertilization,
green tomatoes grow.
Vine stems carry water
and nutrients to the tomatoes.

Ripening

After two to three months,
the tomatoes ripen.
They are picked off the vine.
Seeds inside tomatoes can
grow into new tomato plants.

pumpkin

squash

watermelon

18

Other Foods

Other food ripens on vines.
Pumpkins, squash, and
watermelons grow on vines
along the ground.

pole beans

cucumber

grapes

Pole beans, cucumbers, and grapes also grow on vines. Vines give vegetables and fruits the nutrients they need to grow big and ripe.

Glossary

fertilize—to start seed growth in a plant

nutrient—something that is needed by plants to stay strong and healthy

pollen—tiny yellow grains that flowers make

ripen—to become ready to be harvested, picked, or eaten

seedling—a young plant that has grown from a seed

soil—earth in which plants grow

sprout—to begin to grow

stake—a pointed post that can be driven into the ground; tomato vines can grow upward on stakes

vine—a plant with a long stem that clings to the ground, a stake, or a fence as it grows

Read More

Schuh, Mari. *Growing a Garden.* Gardens. Mankato, Minn.: Capstone Press, 2010.

Snyder, Inez. *Tomatoes.* Harvesttime. New York: Children's Press, 2004.

Whitehouse, Patricia. *Plant and Prune.* Tool Kit. Vero Beach, Fla.: Rourke Pub., 2007.

Internet Sites

FactHound offers a safe, fun way to find Internet sites related to this book. All of the sites on FactHound have been researched by our staff.

Here's all you do:

Visit *www.facthound.com*

Type in this code: 9781429652780

Check out projects, games and lots more at
www.capstonekids.com

23

Index

Word Count: 160
Grade: 1
Early-Intervention Level: 21

Editorial Credits
Erika L. Shores, editor; Bobbie Nuytten, designer; Wanda Winch, media researcher; Laura Manthe, production specialist

Photo Credits
Capstone Press: Karon Dubke, 6 (top left, middle), 8 (inset), 12, 14, 18 (top, middle), 20 (middle); Shutterstock: Antonio S., 6 (bottom), Benis Arapovic, cover (green leaf element), Elena Moiseeva, 8, Igor Zh., 10, Katharina Wittfeld, 4, pokku, 18 (bottom), Sherri R. Camp, 20 (bottom), Stefan Fierros, 20 (top), Tim Ackroyd, 6 (top right), Velychko, 16, Yellowj, cover (red tomato element used throughout book)

The author dedicates this book to her husband, Joe Quam.